Kate McVeigh

12 Ways
TO BE
A BLESSING
TO
Your Church

How to move beyond the ordinary and make an extraordinary impact on your local church.

12 Ways
TO BE
A BLESSING
TO
Your Church

Kate McVeigh

Second Printing 2004

ISBN 0-89276-967-X

In the U.S. write:
Kenneth Hagin Ministries
P.O. Box 50126
Tulsa, OK 74150-0126
1-888-28-FAITH
www.rhema.org

In Canada write:
Kenneth Hagin Ministries
P.O. Box 355, Station D
Etobicoke (Toronto), Ontario
Canada, M9A 4X3

Table of Contents

Introduction

Congratulations! The fact that you are reading this introduction is proof positive that it is your desire to be a blessing to your church in any way you possibly can. You care about people and have a true desire to reach out and help those who are lost and hurting. You are the kind of person God can truly bless!

Anytime we do something for God by helping in our church, He notices our acts of kindness, and they will not go unrewarded by Him. It reminds me of the following scripture that I believe will be true concerning you, because you have already proven your heart's motive by bettering yourself through reading this book.

Hebrews 6:10 AMPLIFIED
For God is not unrighteous to forget or overlook your labor and the love which you have shown for His name's sake in ministering to the needs of the saints (His own consecrated people), as you still do.

It is my desire to motivate you and help you see the joy and benefits in giving to others. Yes, it may often be difficult to deal with people. The devil may have even tried to discourage you from serving in your church in the past, or caused hurt from someone who didn't understand your heart. But God is able to heal any broken relationship and cause you to rise strong again.

The enemy fights us hard, especially where church is concerned, because he knows the difference we are making, and the difference God's Word will make in our life.

I am excited about your love for God's people. I truly believe that when someone is saved in your church or touched by God's love, you will share in the rewards when we all get to Heaven. The reason is, you helped make it possible by doing your part in the Kingdom of God.

I want to thank every one of you who has served faithfully in your church, and you who support ministries with your time, prayers, love, and finances.

I also want to thank anyone reading this book who may have helped my own ministry in any way. You will never know how much your love encourages me to "keep on keeping on" for God. People like you make it all worth it. I believe your pastor feels the same way. It is my prayer that when our work on earth is done, we will both hear the Lord say to us, "Well done, thou good and faithful servant."

Way 1

Ask Not What Your Church Can Do for You, but What You Can Do for Your Church

Do you remember a statement similar to this one made by President John F. Kennedy? In his inaugural address on January 20, 1961, he said, "Ask not what your country can do for you — ask what you can do for your country. My fellow citizens of the world: ask not what America will do for you, but what together we can do for the freedom of man."

I remember learning that famous quote in school. I think more people would be saved and ministered to if Christians had that same thinking in the Church today.

Many times we have a tendency to look for ways to be blessed rather than looking for ways to be a blessing. Of course, you know as well as I do that the best way to have joy unspeakable in our lives is to be a giver. Real joy is in putting others first instead of ourselves.

Acts 20:35 AMPLIFIED
The Lord Jesus . . . Himself said, It is more blessed (makes one happier and more to be envied) to give than to receive.

If you really want to be blessed and get the most out of your church, start looking for ways you can serve. Just imagine what your church would be like if everyone's goal was to be your pastor's biggest blessing. It's going to take all of us working together and each one of us doing our part in these last days to usher in the great harvest of souls.

Ecclesiastes 4:12
A threefold cord is not quickly broken.

There's power in unity and in working together. Your pastor can't do it alone — he needs your help! The following is a humorous story I ran across that talks about how hard it is to do a job alone. I thought it was pretty funny, and that you might enjoy it.

TRYING TO DO THE JOB ALONE

Dear Sir:

I am writing in response to your request for additional information for my insurance claim. In block number three of the accident claim form, I wrote, "trying to do the job alone" as the cause of my accident. You said in your letter that I should explain that statement more fully. I trust the following details will be sufficient.

I am a bricklayer by trade. On the date of the accident, I was working alone on the roof of a new six-story building. When I completed my work I discovered that I had about 500 pounds of brick left over. Rather than carrying the bricks down by hand, I decided to lower them in a barrel by using a pulley which was attached to the side of the building at the sixth-floor level.

Securing the rope at ground level, I went up to the roof, swung the barrel out, and loaded the bricks into it. Then I went back to the ground and untied the rope, holding it tightly to ensure a slow descent of the 500 pounds of bricks. You will note in block number 22 of the claim form that my weight is 175 pounds.

Due to my surprise at being jerked off the ground so suddenly, I lost my presence of mind and forgot to let go of the rope. Needless to say, I proceeded up the side of the building at a very rapid rate of speed.

In the vicinity of the third floor, I met the barrel coming down. This explains my fractured skull and collarbone. Slowed only slightly, I continued my rapid ascent, not stopping until the fingers of my right hand were two knuckles deep into the pulley.

By this time, I had regained my presence of mind and was able to hold tightly to the rope in spite of my pain. At approximately the same time, however, the barrel of bricks hit the ground and the bottom fell out of the barrel. Devoid of the weight of the bricks, the barrel then weighed approximately 50 pounds.

I refer you again to the information in block number 22 regarding my weight. As you might imagine, I began a rapid descent down the side of the building. In the vicinity of the third floor, I met the barrel coming up. This accounts for the two fractured ankles and the lacerations of my legs and lower body.

This second encounter with the barrel slowed me enough to lessen my injuries when I fell onto the pile of bricks, and fortunately, only three vertebrae were cracked.

I am sorry to report, however, that as I lay there on the bricks in pain, unable to stand, and watching the empty barrel six stories above me, I again lost my presence of mind, and let go of the rope. The empty barrel weighed more than the rope so it came down upon me and broke both of my legs.

I hope I have furnished information sufficient to explain why "trying to do the job alone" was the stated cause of the accident.

Sincerely,

A Bricklayer

(Author Unknown)

Working Together Makes Things Better

Have you heard the saying, "Many hands make light work?" How true it is!

I once read a statement that said, "There's no telling what we could accomplish for the Kingdom of God if no one cared who got the credit."

Think about how powerful things could be in your church if everyone was heading in the same direction in one accord, not caring who got the credit.

Powerful things happened in the Book of Acts when the people were all in one accord and laid down their life for the Church. There are a few things that really stand out to me that showed their commitment. Acts chapter 2 says they were all in one accord. And then in Acts chapter 4 when they prayed, the whole building shook. Now that's power!

Acts 4:31 NEW KING JAMES VERSION
**And when they had prayed, the place where they
were assembled together was shaken; and they were
all filled with the Holy Spirit, and they spoke the
word of God with boldness.**

Another thing that stands out to me is the fact that they
were so committed, they even sold their possessions
because the church had needs. That
would be the same as running home
from church and selling your DVD
player, laptop, and big screen TV
just to sow the money to your
church! Wow! You talk about commitment!

> There's no telling
> what we could
> accomplish for the
> Kingdom of God if
> no one cared who
> got the credit.

Now I'm not saying that you
have to go home and do that. I'm just illustrating a point.
The following passage says it all.

Acts 4:32-35 NEW KING JAMES VERSION
**Now the multitude of those who believed were of
one heart and one soul; neither did anyone say that
any of the things he possessed was his own, but they
had all things in common. And with great power the
apostles gave witness to the resurrection of the Lord
Jesus. And great grace was upon them all. Nor was
there anyone among them who lacked; for all who
were possessors of lands or houses sold them, and
brought the proceeds of the things that were sold,**

and laid them at the apostles' feet; and they distributed to each as anyone had need.

Notice what happened as a result of their commitment. *No one lacked!* When you give to God by blessing your church, He will make sure you are taken care of. You can't outgive God!

WHAT I CAN DO FOR MY CHURCH

Instead of criticizing, I will notice the good things about my church:

1. My pastor is a good preacher.

2. I am being fed the Word of God.

3. I enjoy worshiping with other believers.

4. _____

5. _____

6. _____

7. _____

8. _____

9. _____

10. _____

I will not be a part of the problem; I will be part of the solution. The following are some things I can do to be a positive influence in my church:

WHAT I CAN DO	HOW I CAN DO IT
1. Pray for my church and for every service.	I'll pray Saturday night before bed and in my car on the way to church.
2. Pray that more souls are won to the Lord through my church.	I'll pray that the Lord will draw the lost to my church. When the Lord brings someone to mind, I will act immediately by praying for them.
3. Instead of complaining that people are not friendly, I will become friendly at church.	I will introduce myself to people sitting near me, as an example to others. I will seek out those who are alone or who may be there for the first time. I will make them feel welcome by inviting them to sit with me.
4. I will become involved in the ministry of helps by becoming a volunteer.	Next Sunday I will inquire about serving in whatever way I can.

Create your own list here of things you can do
for your local church:

1. _____

2. _____

3. _____

4. _____

5. _____

6. _____

7. _____

8. _____

9. _____

10. _____

Way 2
___

Pray Daily for Your Pastor

I f you really want to get the most out of church, pray for your pastor and his family every day. Pray that God will give him wisdom and keep him strong. Ask the Lord to give him the right message every time he speaks. If you see something in your church or something about your pastor that you don't agree with, pray! Instead of talking about the problem, you should pray. Ask God what you can do to be a blessing.

Your Pastor Is Only Human

We have to realize that pastors are people too. They're human; they are not perfect. They have flaws just like you and me. You know, sometimes ministers have a bad day, just like you do. They don't always do everything right — that's why we should "cut them some slack" and pray for them.

You may think your pastor is not friendly, but the truth could be that he's just shy. While he's preaching under the anointing, he may come across as confident and bold. However, when he is not under the anointing, he might have to work at being more outgoing.

For example, when I am preaching, I often come across as very outgoing, confident, and as though nothing ever bothers me. I can be speaking in front of 5,000 people and seem very comfortable, and I am. However, there are times when I am out of my element — in new situations or in meeting people for the first time. Sometimes I can be in a room with only three or four people, yet I may be nervous.

To tell you truth, I am kind of shy at first around people I don't know well. That has surprised some of my closest friends, but it just goes to show that we're all human. We should always treat ministers with respect (as a matter of fact, the Bible says in First Timothy 5:17 that they're worthy of double honor). But at the same time, we should understand that they are not perfect.

Some people have the idea that all ministers ever do is pray, read their Bible, and study 24 hours a day. I'll never forget the time someone called me on the phone and asked, "Are you studying? Are you praying? Are you fasting today?" I said, "No, I'm eating popcorn and watching '*Little House on the Prairie*'!" I couldn't believe how shocked she was! She had this idea that all I ever did was read the Bible and pray!

> We should always treat ministers with respect. First Timothy 5:17 says they are worthy of double honor.

I heard about one person who saw his pastor playing golf and wearing a golf hat and it freaked him out, so to speak. I guess he thought that all his pastor ever wore was a suit and tie and that he never did anything fun!

Actually, it is scriptural for our lives to be balanced. The Lord wants us to pray, work, rest, and have a proper amount of recreation. We, including your pastor, need to be balanced in every area. God wants us to enjoy our lives! First Timothy 6:17 says that God gives us richly all things to enjoy.

Take It to the Throne, Not to the Phone

Sometimes when you see things that aren't quite right in your church, you may have a tendency to talk about it. Negative things may irritate you, and your concerns may even be legitimate. However, it is never our place to speak negatively or gossip about our pastor, church, or leadership. We don't ever want to be used by the enemy to cause trouble or harm in our church. I'm sure all of us have said things at times that we wish we hadn't said, so the best thing to do is ask God to forgive us and never do it again.

Never let the devil draw you into the trap of gossiping about your pastor. Have you ever heard of "roast pastor"? That means people have the pastor for lunch! In other words, instead of looking at the positive things, they roast the pastor at lunchtime after church by picking apart all the things they didn't agree with in the service.

If They Gossip To You,
They Gossip About You

Have you ever been around certain people that seem to try to pull gossip out of you? Those kinds of people that make you feel as though you have to repent after you leave their presence, because they're always talking negatively about their church or pastor? The Bible is very clear about avoiding these types of people. As a matter of fact, you should run from those who gossip and cause division.

> **Romans 16:17**
> **Now I beseech you, brethren, mark them which cause divisions and offences contrary to the doctrine which ye have learned; and avoid them.**

Notice that this scripture says to mark them *and avoid them*. To mark them simply means to know who they are (and, usually, you know!). Then notice it says *avoid* them, not to think you're better than them, or talk about them. Just don't spend a lot of time with them. Pray for them instead.

The Bible is very serious about those who cause division. As a matter of fact, the Lord can't stand it. He actually hates it, and those are some pretty strong words! Proverbs chapter 6 talks about the seven things the Lord hates, and verse 19 says He hates, *"One who sows discord among brethren"* (NKJV). I don't know

> The Bible is very serious about those who cause division.

about you, but I wouldn't want to have to answer to the Lord for having sown discord or for having been a part of sowing strife by saying the wrong thing.

Here are some other things the Bible says about gossiping and causing division:

Proverbs 16:28 THE LIVING BIBLE
An evil man sows strife; gossip separates the best of friends.

Proverbs 18:8
The words of a talebearer are as wounds . . .

Proverbs 26:20
. . . Where there is no talebearer, the strife ceaseth.

Don't let others gossip to you. My mom always told me when I was growing up, "If people gossip *to* you, they gossip *about* you."

Truthfully, most people who gossip and complain really aren't praying, anyway, and those who pray don't usually gossip or complain! When you get in the Presence of God, He changes *you*. When you pray for your pastor, it will cause the anointing in your church services to increase.

I WILL PRAY OVER MY PASTOR AND HIS FAMILY

My pastor:

My pastor's spouse:

[Insert photo of your pastor and his family.]

Children (and ages):

I have pictures of my spiritual mentors throughout my home and office reminding me to pray for them. You can insert a picture of your pastor and his family as a reminder to pray for them. Cut it out of the church bulletin or use their Christmas picture.

Praying the Word Over Your Pastor

It's important that we pray God's Word and His will, not *our* will, over our pastor. Sometimes people have a tendency to pray things over their pastor, such as, "Lord, change this or that about my pastor," or "Lord, make him not preach so long," and so forth. The truth is, the things you think may need to be changed may not be the things that need changing at all. That's why it's important to pray *God's* will over him instead of your own. The following are some scriptural ways you can pray for your pastor.

> It's important that we pray God's Word and *His* will, not *our* will, over our pastor.

Prayer for Insight and Revelation

Father, I thank You for my pastor. I lift him up before You and ask You to bless him. Give him insight and revelation, so that he will know spiritual truths. Help him to know You more and more. Open the eyes of his heart to see clearly all that You have planned for him and all that You want him to do. Let him know how much You love him and that the greatness of Your power is toward him every day.

Ephesians 1:16-19 — [I] Cease not to give thanks for you, making mention of you in my prayers; that the God of our Lord Jesus Christ, the Father of glory, may give unto you the spirit of wisdom and revelation in the knowledge of him: the eyes of your understanding being enlightened; that ye may know what is the hope of his calling, and what the riches of the glory of his inheritance in the saints, and what is the exceeding greatness of his power to us-ward who believe.

Prayer for Help in Preaching the Word

Father, I pray that my pastor will speak words that come straight from Your throne. Give him boldness and utterance to preach the truth that will make people free and help them to see Jesus as He really is so they can be saved, healed, delivered, and blessed. Let Your strong anointing rest upon him so that as he's preaching and ministering, yokes will be destroyed, burdens will be removed, and lives will be forever changed!

Ephesians 6:19 — And [pray] for me, that utterance may be given unto me, that I may open my mouth boldly, to make known the mystery of the gospel.

Colossians 4:3 — Withal praying also for us, that God would open unto us a door of utterance, to speak the mystery of Christ, for which I am also in bonds.

Isaiah 10:27 — And it shall come to pass in that day, that his burden shall be taken away from off thy shoulder, and his yoke from off thy neck, and the yoke shall be destroyed because of the anointing.

Prayer for Blessing

Father, I pray that my pastor will hear Your voice clearly, and because of that, he will be blessed. Father, according to Your promises, overtake my pastor with blessings! I declare that he is blessed everywhere he goes. His children and all his family are blessed. His household is blessed — their cupboards and refrigerator are always full; they always have more than enough of everything in their house. Lord, may my pastor and his family wear the best, drive the best, and live in the best. Because of Isaiah 1:19, he will eat the good of the land. Give him his heart's desire. Every time he comes in or goes out, he is blessed. Father, I pray that his checking account, savings accounts, and investments are blessed. I declare that everything he sets his hand to is blessed!

Deuteronomy 28:1-8 — And it shall come to pass, if thou shalt hearken diligently unto the voice of the Lord thy God, to observe and to do all his commandments which I command thee this day, that the Lord thy God will set thee on high above all nations of the earth: And all these blessings shall come on thee, and overtake thee, if thou shalt hearken unto the voice of the Lord thy God. Blessed shalt thou be in the city, and blessed shalt thou be in the field. Blessed shall be the fruit of thy body, and the fruit of thy ground, and the fruit of thy cattle, the increase of thy kine, and the flocks of thy sheep. Blessed shall be thy basket and thy store. Blessed shalt thou be when thou comest in, and blessed shalt thou be when thou goest out. The Lord shall cause thine enemies that rise up against thee to be smitten before thy face: they shall come out against thee one way, and flee before thee seven ways. The Lord shall command the blessing upon thee in thy storehouses, and in all that thou settest thine hand unto; and he shall bless thee in the land which the Lord thy God giveth thee.

Isaiah 1:19 — If ye be willing and obedient, ye shall eat the good of the land.

Prayer for Divine Appointments

Father, I pray that you would help my pastor always be in the right place at the right time, with the right people, doing the right thing. Guide his every step so that he can be blessed and be a blessing everywhere he goes. Bring the right people to his church and surround him with people who will encourage him.

Psalm 37:23 — The steps of a good man are ordered by the Lord: and he delighteth in his way.

Prayer for Every Need To Be Met

Father, I pray that You would meet every need in my pastor's life and in the lives of his family — emotional, physical, financial, and spiritual. You know exactly what they need, Father, and I trust You to meet every need in abundance. Surround my pastor with quality people. Thank You for providing all the money, wisdom, help, and equipment needed to carry out Your vision for the church. Thank You for being the God who is more than enough in my pastor's life!

Philippians 4:19 — My God shall supply all your need according to his riches in glory by Christ Jesus.

2 Corinthians 9:8 AMP — And God is able to make all grace (every favor and earthly blessing) come to you in abundance, so that you may always and under all circumstances and whatever the need be self-sufficient [possessing enough to require no aid or support and furnished in abundance for every good work and charitable donation].

Prayer for Protection

Father, I pray for Your protection upon my pastor and his family. Thank You that no matter where they go, Your angels go with them. No plan of the enemy can come to fruition in their lives, for You are always keeping them safe from harm. I declare that while weapons may be formed against them, *none* of those weapons can ever prosper. I ask for Your protection against gossip and slanderous things being spoken against my pastor and his family, for they are the righteousness of God in Christ, and any tongue that rises against them shall be condemned. Thank You that they are supernaturally, divinely protected by the power of Almighty God.

Psalm 91:10,11 — There shall no evil befall thee, neither shall any plague come nigh thy dwelling. For he shall give his angels charge over thee, to keep thee in all thy ways.

Isaiah 54:17 — No weapon that is formed against thee shall prosper; and every tongue that shall rise against thee in judgment thou shalt condemn. This is the heritage of the servants of the Lord, and their righteousness is of me, saith the Lord.

Prayer for Supernatural Wisdom and Holy Spirit Guidance

Father, I ask You to give my pastor supernatural wisdom in dealing with people. I thank You that people will be drawn to Your wisdom in him, and they will be helped because he speaks Your words and conveys Your heart to them. Let him know Your will so he can lead others by Your strength in him. Holy Spirit, You are our helper, and I pray that You will guide my pastor and help him in making decisions. Thank You for showing him things to come so he can deal wisely in the affairs of our church.

John 16:13 — Howbeit when he, the Spirit of truth, is come, he will guide you into all truth: for he shall not speak of himself; but whatsoever he shall hear, that shall he speak: and he will shew you things to come.

James 1:5 — If any of you lack wisdom, let him ask of God, that giveth to all men liberally, and upbraideth not; and it shall be given him.

Colossians 1:9 — . . . [I] do not cease to pray for you, and to desire that ye might be filled with the knowledge of his will in all wisdom and spiritual understanding.

Prayer for the Gifts of the Spirit To Flow Freely

Father, thank You for the gifts of the Spirit that You have given to our church to profit all of us. Thank You for helping my pastor be even more sensitive to the moving of Your Spirit. Stir him up every day to desire spiritual gifts, and cause them to flow freely through him and our church to help and bless the people.

1 Corinthians 12:7-11 — The manifestation of the Spirit is given to every man to profit withal. For to one is given by the Spirit the word of wisdom; to another the word of knowledge by the same Spirit; to another faith by the same Spirit; to another the gifts of healing by the same Spirit; to another the working of miracles; to another prophecy; to another discerning of spirits; to another divers kinds of tongues; to another the interpretation of tongues: But all these worketh that one and the selfsame Spirit, dividing to every man severally as he will.

1 Corinthians 14:1 — Follow after charity, and desire spiritual gifts . . . .

The Prayers of Paul

This is one of the best ways you can pray for your pastor and his wife. Put your pastor's name in the blanks.

Ephesians 1:16-19

I cease not to give thanks for Pastor _____ and

_____, making mention of them in my prayers; that the

God of my Lord Jesus Christ, the Father of glory, may give

unto Pastor _____ and _____ the spirit of wisdom

and revelation in the knowledge of Him: the eyes of their

understanding being enlightened; that they may know what

is the hope of their calling, and what the riches of the glory

of His inheritance in the saints, and what is the exceeding

greatness of His power toward Pastor _____ and

_____ who believe, according to the working of His

mighty power.

Ephesians 3:14-19

I bow my knees unto the Father of our Lord Jesus Christ, of

whom the whole family in heaven and earth is named, that

He would grant Pastor _____ and _____, according

to the riches of His glory, to be strengthened with might by

His Spirit in the inner man; that Christ may dwell in Pastor

_____'s and _____'s heart by faith; that Pastor

_____ and _____, being rooted and grounded in love,

may be able to comprehend with all saints what is the

breadth, and length, and depth, and height; and to know the

love of Christ, which passeth knowledge, that they might be

filled with all the fulness of God.

Philippians 1:9-11

And this I pray, that Pastor _____'s and _____'s love may abound yet more and more in knowledge and in all judgment; that Pastor _____ and _____ may approve things that are excellent; that they may be sincere and without offense til the day of Christ; being filled with the fruits of righteousness, which are by Jesus Christ, unto the glory and praise of God.

Colossians 1:9-11

I do not cease to pray for Pastor _____ and _____, and to desire that they might be filled with the knowledge of His will in all wisdom and spiritual understanding; that Pastor _____ and _____ might walk worthy of the Lord unto all pleasing, being fruitful in every good work, and increasing in the knowledge of God; strengthened with all might, according to His glorious power, unto all patience and long-suffering with joyfulness.

Way 3

Bless Your Pastor on
Special Occasions

1 Timothy 5:17
Let the elders that rule well be counted worthy of
double honour, especially they who labour in the
word and doctrine.

The fact that you are reading this book is proof positive that you love your pastor and that you respect men and women of God in the ministry. Often ministers go unappreciated by the world. In the world, people do not understand the value of spiritual leadership. A good shepherd gives his life for the sheep (John 10:11). Nothing is more important than our spiritual well-being. The Bible says in Ephesians 4:11 that our pastors are a gift from God.

One day I was reflecting about the value of spiritual leadership and how it has affected my own life. I was thinking about a minister who had such a huge impact on me and my entire family. As a result of this particular ministry, I was saved and my life was completely changed, going from despair and hopelessness as a young teenager to happiness, hope, and a bright future. This minister's obedience to

God made all the difference in the world to me. I could never express in words how much this minister means to me, and there's no amount of money I could give to repay what was sown into my life.

However, the Bible says in John 3:16 that giving is one of the chief expressions of love. It says, *"For God so loved the world that He GAVE. . . ."* What did God give? His very best. God did not just look at the world and say, "I love you"; He did something about it. Even though money and words can't match how you feel, they sure can be a blessing and an encouragement to someone who has blessed your life spiritually. If you really love and appreciate someone, you should express it by giving.

> If you really love and appreciate someone, you should express it by giving.

Giving is not just monetary. It *can* be money; however, there are also other ways to give. Your pastor should be celebrated! Just think about how people in the world celebrate musicians, movie stars, and athletes. What your pastor is doing is so much more important than what these people do! He is affecting lives for eternity. That is why I believe it is vitally important to be a blessing to your pastor, especially on special occasions.

Celebrate Your Pastor

A great way to celebrate and be a blessing to your pastor and his wife is to simply let them know that you appreciate them! This can be done with words of appreciation — by expressing verbally or with a written note how much they mean to you and your family. You can do this throughout the year.

Then there are special occasions. You always want to remember them on their special days, such as Father's Day and Mother's Day, birthdays, anniversaries, and so forth. It would really be a blessing if you put some money in the card too! Pastors rarely get paid what they are worth. You may not realize it, but many times, they are believing God for extra money.

I preach all over the country several times a week, and most churches I preach in receive a special offering to bless their pastors on their anniversaries, birthdays, and other special occasions. I'll never forget the time, years ago, when I was in a smaller church, and an offering was received for the pastor because he had an older car. The entire congregation was so excited to give, because the pastor had never had a brand-new vehicle. With less than 100 people, enough money came in to buy him a brand-new car. Praise God! I was so glad to be there so I could get in on sowing that wonderful seed into his life.

Of course, guess what happened in that church as a result? People started getting blessed! Many of them shared testimonies of supernaturally receiving better or brand-new cars themselves! I was not surprised. You reap what you sow (Gal. 6:7). Several years later, even I was blessed with a brand-new vehicle!

Other Ways To Give

When I talk about giving, as I said, there are other ways you can give besides just giving money.

For example, when I was a teenager, I didn't have any money to give my pastor for his birthday. I really wanted to be a blessing, but had nothing to give him, not even a dime! So I set aside my embarrassment and asked the Lord to help me come up with something to sow. I wrote a letter telling my pastor and his wife how much I appreciated them both, and in place of money (because I didn't have any to give at the time), I was sowing a seed of prayer. I got creative and made up a little gift certificate that read, "One half hour of prayer every day for two weeks." I also took time to write him a poem and it is hanging on his office wall to this day. He told me that was the best birthday present he had ever received, because it came from the heart.

> There are other ways you can give besides just giving money.

How To Be a Blessing

If you have an idea for blessing your pastor on a special occasion, you should check with your pastor's spouse or someone else in authority at the church to share your idea.

It's important to go through the proper channels when you have an idea such as receiving an offering or buying something special for your pastor. A lot of people mean well, but then their idea backfires and is not a blessing because they didn't go about it the right way.

There are several reasons why. One reason may be that someone in leadership may already have a plan in the making along the same lines as your idea. Another reason may be that when it comes to giving money for certain things, you may have to check into the legal side of the issue, and it's better to do that through the leadership in your church. Another reason is, what if every church member went around collecting money from other members every time he or she had a good idea? Then your pastor would be cleaning up a mess, and it wouldn't be a blessing to him or your church! It would just be added work to establish order out of chaos.

If no one is excited about your idea, or you don't seem to be getting anywhere with it, then just go ahead and bless your pastor as best you can. Send your own appreciation card and be generous.

Of course, never forget how hard your pastor's wife works in the ministry as well. She can often be overlooked. My pastor's wife has made a tremendous impact on my life and ministry. She has been a wonderful example of a virtuous woman, and her influence in our church has made all the difference in the world. She's a wonderful role model for women; she should be celebrated and appreciated. And believe me, women like to be appreciated!

What you help make happen for a man or woman of God, God can make happen for you.

> What you help make happen for a man or woman of God, God can make happen for you.

If you remember others on their special days, God can cause others to remember you on your special days. When you bless someone else, you can be blessed in return.

INFORMATION I NEED TO KNOW TO BLESS MY PASTOR

My pastor's birthday is:

My pastor's spouse's birthday is:

My pastor's anniversary is:

The church's anniversary is:

My pastor's favorite restaurant is:

My pastor's favorite hobby/pastime is:

My pastor's favorite way to relax is:

My pastor's favorite treat is:

My pastor's spouse's favorite hobby/pastime is:

My pastor's spouse's favorite way to relax is:

My pastor's spouse's favorite treat is:

IDEAS FOR BLESSING YOUR PASTORS
ON SPECIAL OCCASIONS

1. Buy a gift certificate to their favorite restaurant.

2. Send a note saying how much you'll pray for them.

3. Bless them with money (so they can get what they want).

4. Buy a mall gift certificate.

5. Offer to clean their house or baby-sit (for smaller churches).

6. Offer to clean the church or mow the lawn (for smaller churches).

7. Help set up and tear down equipment (if applicable).

Create your own list here:

8. _____

9. _____

10. _____

11. _____

12. _____

13. _____

14. _____

15. _____

Way 4

Get Involved in the
Helps Ministry

A great way to be a blessing to your church is to serve in the ministry of helps. If you really want to be a blessing, then be available for anything your pastor needs to make the church run smoothly.

Helps ministry simply means "to *help*" in any way that help is needed. It's important that you do what helps your pastor the most and not just what *you* think he needs. It's kind of like buying someone a birthday present. You may really like it, but it doesn't mean the other person will like it as much as you do. The best thing to do is to find out what that person really likes and get him what *he* wants. Even if it's not what we like, it's a much bigger blessing.

> It's important that you do what helps your pastor the most and not just what *you* think he needs.

Back Your Pastor's Vision

We must remember that it is our job to back the vision God has given to our pastor. Sometimes people tend to promote their *own* vision instead of backing their pastor's vision, not realizing that it is his vision that counts the most in your church.

You may have a great idea for something you think your church should do, but you should understand that your pastor may not feel called to do that, or the church is already doing everything it can and can't take on another project. But if you have a great idea, there are some things you can do. You can pray about it, or you can volunteer to start it and keep it running. One reason pastors don't always go for a great idea is, people often have great ideas, but they'll bail out of it after three months, and the church gets stuck running it. Often we must prove ourselves faithful before the church leadership will accept our ideas.

Be Open To Help Anywhere

The best thing you can do is make yourself available for any position, wherever help is needed. Often you will start out in one area of helps ministry, but end up somewhere else. You may have a heart to be in one position, but there's not an opening there yet. I believe God will honor your act of obedience and willingness to help, even if your area of service is not your ultimate desire. You should be honest with your leaders by letting them know what you really have a heart for, but that you are open and willing to do something else for now if there is a need.

For example, when I was a teenager, before I went into full-time ministry, I worked in the children's department for about five years. I did puppets, skits, learned how to juggle, and became "Katie the Clown." The kids loved it! I studied like crazy and worked for hours with our team so the skits would be perfect on Sunday morning, and the kids were really ministered to.

Never look at your job as "just children's ministry" or "just youth ministry." You are making a difference and changing lives! Now, in my heart I didn't feel I would always minister to kids; I felt called to a traveling ministry. However, I knew that I needed to be faithful in this area if I expected to have a ministry of my own one day.

Proverbs 28:20
A faithful man shall abound with blessings. . . .

When I was helping in children's ministry, I knew that I was sowing seeds for my future. If I sowed seeds of faithfulness, then I would reap faithful people to help me. I also learned that if you can keep the attention of kids, you can preach anywhere!

You probably won't start out where you desire to ultimately be, but if you remain faithful, God will promote you.

Psalm 75:6,7
For promotion cometh neither from the east, nor from the west, nor from the south. But God is the judge: he putteth down one, and setteth up another.

If you really want to be a blessing — and I know you do or you wouldn't be reading this book — then make yourself available any place there is a need, and this could even include cleaning the restrooms. In my church, if there was a need, I tried my best to fill it. I even learned how to play the drums because we needed a drummer!

Be Part of the Solution

One minister friend of mine always says, "You will be remembered in life either by the problems you solve for others or by the ones you create."

Just think about it. Even at work, we are rewarded for solving problems. Surgeons solve physical problems, accountants solve tax problems, judges solve legal problems, bus drivers solve transportation problems, cooks solve hunger problems, and on and on. Everywhere you go, you're either creating or solving a problem. You want your pastor to notice you for the problems you solve, not the ones you create.

For example, when the service starts and there are not enough people to help in the nursery, the approved nursery worker who gets up and goes in to help has solved a problem.

People need you when they need you and where they need you, even if it is not convenient for you. If they need you "right now" in the nursery, it does not help them if you say you're available in two weeks. I've had people say, "I'll volunteer for you, but I won't do this or that . . . ." In other words, they'll usher, but they won't greet. Or they'll say, "I'll help you in any way, but I'm busy this week — let me know next time." That's not solving my immediate problems.

Problem solvers are usually the ones who end up getting promoted. Why is that? Because they're relieving stress on their pastor by solving a problem. God can promote you when you're part of the answer, not the problem.

Hold Up Your Pastor's Arms

In Exodus 17, Moses and the children of Israel fought a battle against the Amalekites. Moses, the leader, and his two helpers, Aaron and Hur, went to the top of a hill to watch the battle, and when Moses held up his hands, the Israelites prevailed over their enemies. But when his arms got tired and he lowered them, the Amalekites prevailed.

So Aaron and Hur rushed to aid Moses, holding up his arms so the battle could be won. Exodus 17:12 and 13 says, "*. . . and his hands were steady until the going down of the sun. So Joshua defeated Amalek and his people with the edge of the sword.*"

The Israelites won their battle when someone helped to hold up the arms of the leader.

That is what can happen in your church too. Your pastor can't do everything himself. When helps ministers hold up

> People need you when they need you and where they need you, even if it is not convenient for you.

his arms by doing the work of the ministry in the church, the whole congregation can win battles and many souls to the Lord.

Notice this scripture also says they held up his arms until the sun went down. That means they stuck with Moses, holding up his arms even when things were hard. They didn't give out before the job was done. They didn't quit just because the day grew long and things became difficult. They stood behind their leader and, together, won a great victory. Moses could not have done it without them, and they could not have done it without Moses. They needed each other.

Make Your Pastor's Job Easier

The Bible says that the pastor's job is to teach *you and me* how to do the work of the ministry.

Ephesians 4:11
And he gave some, apostles; and some, prophets; and some, evangelists; and some, pastors and teachers; for the perfecting of the saints, for the work of the ministry, for the edifying of the body of Christ.

Your pastor isn't supposed to be doing all the work of the church himself. As a matter of fact, that would be impossible. Things run more smoothly in your church and you can be more effective in reaching others when everyone is doing his part. It should be our goal to free our pastor up from the day-to-day natural duties

> Things run more smoothly in your church and you can be more effective in reaching others when everyone is doing his part.

as much as we can, so he can spend his time praying and studying the Word to feed the congregation.

The Bible talks about the importance of ministers being relieved of natural duties to be able to devote the majority of their attention to spiritual things such as studying, praying, and preparing teachings to feed the flock each week.

In the Book of Acts, the church was growing and everyone was busy. The disciples soon realized they needed help, because they found themselves waiting on tables, doing natural things. They recognized the importance of not neglecting what they were really called to do, which was preaching and teaching the Word of God. The following passage of scripture reveals that your pastor shouldn't always have to be performing the natural duties of the ministry. That's why he needs our help. We come to his aid by holding up his arms, taking the load off him, solving problems for him, and helping in any way we possibly can.

Acts 6:2-4 MESSAGE
They said, "It wouldn't be right for us to abandon our responsibilities for preaching and teaching the Word of God to help with the care of the poor. So, friends, choose seven men from among you whom everyone trusts, men full of the Holy Spirit and good sense, and we'll assign them this task. Meanwhile, we'll stick to our assigned task of prayer and speaking God's Word."

I don't know about you, but I don't want my pastor worn out when Sunday comes around, because he's had to vacuum, clean, and set up chairs the night before. I want him to be prayed up, full of the anointing, and rested so he can speak the life-changing Word of God to every one of us.

Do You Qualify?

Notice the previous passage in Acts talks about the qualifications for helps ministry: they should be people that *"everyone trusts, men full of the Holy Spirit and good sense."* When God chooses people to help, He's looking for these qualities. There are even more qualifications mentioned in First Timothy chapter 3. Let's take a look at some of the other qualifications of key leadership positions in the church.

First Timothy 3:10-13 talks about the qualifications for helps ministry. If you look up different Bible translations of this passage, you will find some of the following things listed. Helps ministers need to:

1. *Be proven faithful first.*
   1 Timothy 3:10 AMPLIFIED
   And let them also be tried and investigated and proved first; then, if they turn out to be above reproach, let them serve [as deacons].

Often people want to jump right into a position. They may even be talented, gifted, and well-prepared for that position. However, the Scripture says we must be proven *faithful* first before entering a key position. Your pastor needs to see first that you are dependable, a person of integrity, and qualified for

> . . . Scripture says we must be proven *faithful* first before entering a key position.

that particular area of ministry. It may take time to prove yourself to your pastor. Don't be discouraged when you are not immediately put into a prominent position of leadership. Your pastor is only being scriptural by seeing your faithfulness first.

2. *Be the husband of one wife.* Basically, that means you are to be a one-woman man (or a one-man woman). *The Message* Bible says, "Servants in the church are to be committed to their spouses and to their own children."

3. *Have your financial affairs in order.* This is speaking of having a good reputation with people. It simply means that you're not known around town for never paying your bills or being late with payments on everything. *The Message* Bible says in First Timothy 3:7 that outsiders are to think well of you.

4. *Be above reproach.* That means you should be a person of integrity. You represent your church (and, more importantly, you represent the Lord) out in public. For example, it isn't right to see a children's worker hanging out at a bar, or one of the married ushers driving around town with a

> Put the past behind and start today by making the necessary adjustments to qualify yourself to be a blessing.

woman other than his spouse. The Bible tells us that we should avoid the appearance of evil (1 Thess. 5:22). This should be our goal at all times. We want to be a good example for the Lord as His representatives.

I Don't Qualify — What Should I Do?

In reading the previous scriptures on qualifications for helps ministry, you may see some areas in which you have failed to qualify. Well, I have good news for you. You can get qualified!

How do you do that? First of all, ask the Lord to forgive you if you see that you have missed it. The Bible says in First John 1:9 that when we confess our sin to God, He forgives us, cleanses us, and acts as though it never existed. So we must receive our forgiveness by faith and begin to qualify ourselves by doing what is right and acting in accordance with the Word of God. Don't let the devil beat you over the head about your mistakes. Put the past behind and start today by making the necessary adjustments to qualify yourself to be a blessing.

Philippians 3:13,14
. . . This one thing I do, forgetting those things which are behind, and reaching forth unto those things which are before, I press toward the mark for the prize of the high calling of God in Christ Jesus.

HOW I CAN FURTHER QUALIFY FOR HELPS MINISTRY

According to First Timothy chapter 3, more qualifications for the ministry of helps are as follows: *(Look in different Bible translations.)*

1. _____

2. _____

3. _____

4. _____

5. _____

Things I can work on in my life to become a more excellent helps minister:

1. I will be on time; I will not be late.

2. I will do the best job I can and strive for excellence.

3. I will listen carefully to and carry out instructions.

4. _____

5. _____

6. _____

7. _____

8. _____

9. _____

10. _____

Areas in which help is most greatly needed in my church:

_____

_____

_____

_____

_____

Areas in which I can start serving now:

_____

_____

_____

_____

_____

Areas in which I feel called to serve:

_____

_____

_____

_____

_____

Way 5

Follow Through
With Commitments

Following through with commitments is a vital part of being a blessing to your church.

There are several vital areas in which following through is important. One is to be committed to your church. By that I mean, once you have found your home church, be faithful to attend there.

There are always new churches popping up in every town, and sometimes people go visit just to see what's happening there. But when your home church is having services, you really should be there in support of your pastor and congregation. There are a lot of "cruise-a-matics" out there! They are people who keep cruising around from church to church, never settling down anywhere long enough to receive all God has for them.

As a traveling minister, I never hold my own special meetings on a Sunday morning. I preach in a local church every Sunday, but I wouldn't hold my own meeting on a church day. I wouldn't want to conflict with or draw people away from their local church.

Make Sure It Will Fit Before You Commit!

I would encourage you to really pray before making a major commitment. Make sure you count the cost before taking the leap. Many people commit to serving in an area before really praying and thinking it through. They get excited about helping and do great at first, but they often don't continue to be faithful.

So always pray before you commit. Be sure to discuss any commitment with your spouse — make sure it's going to fit into your life, with your schedule, your family, and so forth.

On the other hand, sometimes people never commit to anything, and they even use God as an excuse. They'll say, "Well, I don't feel led." Here is an idea that might help you *and* your church out. Your church may have an immediate situation arise in which help is desperately needed. You want to be a blessing, but you're not sure about committing to something long-term. Why not tell your leader that you could help out *temporarily* to address an immediate need? In the mean time, you could be praying about making a long-term commitment.

> Make sure you count the cost before taking the leap.

Psalm 15:4

. . . He honoureth them that fear the Lord. He that sweareth to his own hurt, and changeth not.

Sometimes we have to keep our commitment, even though it may hurt. Have you ever committed to something before you thought about it or prayed about it? Ask me why I'm an expert on this subject! I found out the hard way about speaking before thinking.

One day I was sitting in church, and the pastor was sharing with the congregation the need for a new cordless microphone. This was a small congregation of less than 50 people. The pastor was leading an open discussion about how to go about purchasing a new thousand-dollar microphone. Before I even had time to think, I heard myself saying, "I can believe God for the money to pay for that."

After leaving church that day, I thought I was going to be sick! What was I thinking? Here I was in my first year of Bible school — I didn't even have enough money for tuition, and now I'd just committed to buying a thousand-dollar microphone!

I got to thinking about my options. First, I thought I could just go back to the pastor and tell him that I spoke out of line and that I was really broke. Maybe he would release me of my commitment if he understood my circumstances. And he probably would have.

However, the more I thought about it, I really felt I needed to keep my word — and, next time, *think* before I spoke!

I ended up making monthly payments to the church for the entire year. It was a hard lesson

> Once you do commit . . . you need to keep your word.

for a young person to learn, and I really did swear to my own hurt. But I truly believe the Lord honored my commitment and has blessed me to this day for keeping my word. As a matter of fact, several years later, a church sowed $1,000 for me to buy a cordless microphone for my own ministry!

It's good to pray about things and think them through before you make a major commitment. Once you do commit and give your word, you need to swear to your own hurt and change not. In other words, you need to keep your word.

Don't Drop the Ball

Often when people are volunteering in church, they may tend to think it's not important to follow through with their commitment because they're not getting paid. When people drop the ball, they often don't see how their decisions affect others.

One time I had a big ministry conference planned. We had been working on this conference for months so that everything would be perfect for people when they walked through the doors. We were expecting about 300 people, and we wanted everyone to be ministered to in a powerful way.

I hired some Christians to bring a sound system, set it up, and run it for me. The week before the meeting, my office spoke with them to confirm they would be there early to set things up and work out any glitches before the meeting started. *The day before* our big event, I received a phone call from them saying that they had changed their mind and wouldn't be there!

They didn't stop to think how their decision would affect us and the 300 people that were coming. You can't find a sound system to rent on one day's notice. Our office

> Sometimes we don't realize what we put other people through when we don't keep our word.

staff frantically called every rental place in town, and they all told us the same thing: "You have to reserve a sound system in advance." Nothing was available.

I don't think these people realized the undue stress they put on everyone involved. They had no real reason for not showing up, other than they didn't feel like it.

Of course, we cast our cares on the Lord and prayed. But the fact of the matter is, we shouldn't have had to do that just because some people didn't keep their word. Thank God, a wonderful church came to my rescue and supplied the sound system, microphones, and people to run everything. God is faithful!

Sometimes we don't realize what we put other people through when we don't keep our word. I'm sure those people who cancelled on me had no idea what I went through trying to find a replacement. It would have been better had they never offered to help rather than to have put me and my staff through all that trouble.

It can be the same way when someone doesn't show up to usher or work in the nursery. That leaves others short-handed, people aren't ministered to as effectively, and someone else will probably have to take your place on a moment's notice. Or there may be no one to take your place, which can cause all sorts of problems. We want people to be blessed, not stressed!

I realize there are times when emergencies arise and you can't keep your commitment — that's different. Or once in a while, your leader may allow you to take a break. In that case, make arrangements in advance for someone else to fill in for you. Remember, people are counting on you, and the Bible says that a faithful man will abound with blessings (Prov. 28:20).

Start Today and You'll Be Okay

I haven't said all this to make you feel bad. Maybe there are areas in which you haven't followed through, or you broke your word. If so, I encourage you to start fresh and new today. Purpose in your heart that you will become a person of integrity by keeping your word and following through with your commitments.

The following scriptures are powerful promises to those who are faithful and diligent. Begin to confess these scriptures and see them work in your life.

Proverbs 10:4
He becometh poor that dealeth with a slack hand:
but the hand of the diligent maketh rich.

Father, I will be diligent in working for my church and in everything You give me to do. Therefore, I will not become poor, but will be made rich, according to Your promise.

Proverbs 12:24
The hand of the diligent shall bear rule: but the slothful shall be under tribute.

Father, as I apply myself to be a diligent helper, You will promote me, and I can be a leader of people.

Proverbs 13:4
The soul of the sluggard desireth, and hath nothing: but the soul of the diligent shall be made fat.

Father, thank You that as I work diligently for Your Kingdom, my soul shall be made fat, and I will be abundantly provided for.

Proverbs 21:5
The thoughts of the diligent tend only to plenteousness; but of every one that is hasty only to want.

Because I am diligent, my thoughts tend only to plenty and not to lack.

Proverbs 22:29 MESSAGE
Observe people who are good at their work —
skilled workers are always in demand and admired;
they don't take a back seat to anyone.

Father, I purpose to do my best in everything I do, and I thank You that, as a result, my work will always be in demand.

FOLLOWING THROUGH

The following are some ways I can become more diligent in keeping my commitments:

1. _____

2. _____

3. _____

4. _____

5. _____

6. _____

7. _____

8. _____

9. _____

10. _____

Way 6

Submit With Style
And Always Smile

Yikes! Just seeing that word "submit" makes some people nervous! What do I mean when I say "submit with style"? That means to have a good attitude. According to the dictionary, one meaning of "submit" is *to yield oneself to the authority or will of another; to surrender.*

What I'm talking about is surrendering your way of doing things to the way your leadership wants things done. When speaking of submission it is important to realize that submission and agreement are two entirely different things. You really haven't submitted until you disagree. You know you're truly submitting when it's a little hard on your flesh.

> Surrender your way of doing things to the way your leadership wants things done.

To show you the difference between submission and agreement, let's say your pastor asks you to do something a certain way, and you think it's a great idea. You are in agreement.

However, let's say he asks you to do something a certain way, and you don't think it's a good idea. In other words, if you were in charge, you would never do it that way. *This* is where submission comes in.

At this point, you have a decision to make. The Lord's way of doing it would be to honor your leader by doing it the way he or she want you to, *without complaining.* This is how we submit.

Now it may be true that your way of doing it is actually better. However, if that's not the way your leader wants it done, it doesn't matter what you think. True submission will do it their way, in love. This is what I mean by it being hard on your flesh!

When speaking of submission, it's important that you know that it's never right to submit to something contrary to the Word of God. The Lord would never want you to submit to something that is outside the boundaries of His Word, such as sin or abuse. Some people twist the definition of submission. I've heard of situations in which people were trying so hard to be submissive that they actually let other people abuse them. That is not God's will, and that is *not* the kind of submission I'm referring to.

Passing the Test

Most problems I have seen with submission in local churches usually involve personality conflicts, personal preferences, and the manner or style in which things are done.

For example, when I travel and speak in local churches all over the world, I am to be in submission to that local pastor. My job is to preach the Word and be a blessing. Even though I have my own ministry, when I am speaking in a particular church, I come under the pastor's authority. I may not always agree with his method of doing things, and if I were in charge, I might want to do things a different way. However, it is still my job to do it the way God is leading that pastor because it's his church, and he is the one God has placed in authority over that body of believers.

It would be helpful to you to find out your pastor's likes and dislikes. As an outsider coming in, I don't always know how things are done in that church, so I try to ask a lot of questions in a short amount of time to give me some sort of an idea.

However, as a member of your local church congregation, you have the advantage of being present every week, perhaps for years. (As a matter of fact, by now you ought to know a lot of your pastor's likes and dislikes!) Anybody who has been attending my church for more than a year and doesn't know that my pastor likes to drink IBC root beer hasn't been paying attention (it's a soda pop, for those of you outside the U.S.!). Pay attention to details!

When I'm ministering in a church, I try to find out how long I'm expected to preach, how the pastor likes the altar call done, and so forth. One time, I traveled a long way to minister in a particular church.

> In dealing with people, sometimes you just have to go with the flow and keep your heart right.

After arriving, to my dismay, I was told by the pastor that I had just under 15 minutes to preach! Did I think that was too short? Yes! Did I think it was a waste of my time traveling all that way to minister for such a short time? Yes! Did I think they had wasted their money flying me all the way there for 15 minutes of preaching? Yes! Did I complain about it? No! Did I feel like complaining about it? Yes! Do we go by our feelings? No!

This is where Bible submission comes into play. I did just what they asked me to do, and with a good attitude because it was the right thing to do. In dealing with people, sometimes you just have to go with the flow and keep your heart right.

Guess what happened as a result? A lot of people got saved in that service! The Lord moved powerfully in less than 15 minutes? It's amazing what will happen when you keep your heart right. I "passed the test" that day, and so can you.

The Rewards of Submitting When It's Hard

1 Peter 2:18 NEW KING JAMES VERSION
Servants, be submissive to your masters with all fear [meaning *reverence*], **not only to the good and gentle, but also to the harsh.**

If you look up that word "harsh" in the Greek, it actually means: *unreasonable tyrant.* Have you ever felt like you were working or serving under someone who was acting like an unreasonable tyrant? I'm sure that we have all been there. There may be times when you are working under a difficult leader who is hard to understand. He may have some weaknesses in his flesh that stand out to you. Perhaps you have even seen his shortcomings. This is a real opportunity to walk in love. If you respond the way the Lord wants you to — with humility — blessings will come your way.

Just think about Hannah in the Book of First Samuel, Chapter 1. This is a beautiful story of how Hannah submitted to a leader who was acting unreasonably. As a result of her submission, she received the desire of her heart.

Hannah loved the Lord with all her heart, but was never able to conceive children. All she wanted was to have a child, but it just wasn't happening. She began realizing that God was the answer to this impossible situation. So one day she went to church to pray. She was praying fervently with all her heart. As a matter of fact, she was praying so intensely that her lips were moving but nothing was coming out.

Right about that time, the head priest (or pastor) walked in and saw her praying. All Eli saw were her lips moving with nothing coming out, and because he was not a very good leader, he immediately accused her of being drunk. How insulting! I don't know about you, but I think I may have been tempted to be upset if I were Hannah.

Hannah's reaction to this leader made all the difference in the world. Instead of being offended when he accused her of drinking, she responded with humility. She respected his leadership position. She may not have respected his lifestyle or the lifestyle of his sons (1 Sam. 2:12), but she respected him. She explained to him with humility that she was praying. She even addressed him with a title out of respect when speaking to him(1 Sam. 1:15). (It's good to call your pastor "Pastor," because doing that shows respect.)

> Instead of being offended when he accused her . . . she responded with humility.

Let's read what happened to Hannah as a result of her submitting to authority with a good attitude.

> **1 Samuel 1:17** NEW KING JAMES VERSION
> **Then Eli answered and said, "Go in peace, and the God of Israel grant your petition which you have asked of Him."**

Hannah received the desire of her heart. In less than one year, she had a baby sitting on her lap who ended up bringing deliverance to all of Israel. His name was Samuel, and he grew up to be the priest after Eli.

Talk about restitution! Her own son ended up taking over the job of Eli, the leader who had been mean to her. When you do what's right, right things will happen to you.

WAYS I CAN HAVE A GREAT SUBMISSIVE ATTITUDE

1. I will not be offended when I am corrected.

2. When asked to do something I don't want to do, I will do it with a good attitude.

3. I will not insist upon my own way.

4. _____

5. _____

6. _____

7. _____

8. _____

9. _____

10. _____

Way 7

Recognize the Trap Of Familiarity

Many times when serving pastors or ministry leaders, we become too familiar and let our guard down in respecting their position of authority. What I mean is, once the Lord allows us the place of becoming close to a minister, we may begin to see his or her flaws, faults, and shortcomings. We will begin to see that they are human just like us! Ministers are not perfect.

The Lord may allow you the privilege of being around your leader often and serving him in the "inner circle." Many times when people start in a position like that, they're excited and they consider it to be a tremendous honor to be close to their pastor. But as time goes on and the real work begins, the honeymoon period begins to wear off. They start to realize that ministry is not all glamorous. It is a lot of work. There is much more to ministry than meets the eye.

When you work with someone closely and become familiar with him or her, it's easy to let

> When you work with someone closely and become familiar with him or her, it's easy to let your guard drop.

your guard drop. We have to constantly keep our pastor in the proper place in our hearts and minds. Any time you get closer to someone, you will begin to see their idiosyncrasies or things that they are still overcoming in the flesh. However, don't allow these things to cause you to become too familiar, to the point that you let your honor and respect for them slip. Don't start thinking of them as "just one of the gang." This can be Satan's trap to rob you of receiving from God's anointed.

Honor the Anointing

One reason we are to respect our pastor is because of God's anointing on his life. It's important to separate the man from the anointing and understand that the gift of God can flow through an imperfect vessel. The following scripture tells us that we are all just vessels that God is working through.

2 Corinthians 4:7 MESSAGE
If you only look at us, you might well miss the brightness. We carry this precious Message around in the unadorned clay pots of our ordinary lives. That's to prevent anyone from confusing God's incomparable power with us.

The story of David and Saul is a good example of honoring the anointing on someone's life. In First Samuel chapter 19, King Saul was in a jealous rage, trying to kill David because he had been anointed king in his place. In First Samuel chapter 24, he was pursuing David across the countryside, wanting to kill him. God was replacing Saul as king, and he was not a happy camper! He was yielding to the wrong spirit.

One day David was hiding from Saul in a cave. Suddenly David looked up from his hiding place and saw Saul standing at the doorway of the cave, close enough for David to reach out and kill him.

David had a straight shot at killing Saul, because Saul hadn't seen David. You would think that killing Saul would have solved all of David's problems — he could rightfully take over as king and stop having to flee his pursuer. David could have killed Saul before Saul killed him — after all, he would have just been defending himself.

But David wouldn't do it. Why? Because he knew Saul had been anointed at one time. When his men asked him why he didn't killed Saul when he had the chance, he answered, *"The Lord forbid that I should do this thing unto my master, the Lord's anointed, to stretch forth mine hand against him, seeing he is the anointed of the Lord"* (1 Sam. 24:6).

David wouldn't even talk against Saul years later after he was dead. Talk about not being a gossiper! You'd think it would be okay to talk about someone after they were dead, but David knew better. He didn't get caught in the trap of familiarity, and we don't want to either.

Familiarity Checklist

The following is a checklist to see if you may have become too familiar with your pastor. These are the top ten warning signs that you need a "heart" checkup:

1. You are noticing your leader's faults and starting to judge them in your heart.

2. You are jealous or think that you deserve the same attention, gifts, and money your leader has received.

3. You have a negative attitude when you are asked to do something beyond your job description, but you were more than willing in the beginning.

4. You are defensive or blame someone else when confronted with a mistake you made.

5. You can't stand to be corrected.

6. You often think to yourself that you would do it differently if you were in charge.

7. You always think your way is better.

8. You think it's okay to correct your pastor and you challenge his decisions.

9. You have more than once talked about your pastor behind his back.

10. You have not stood up for your pastor when others have spoken negatively about them.

If any of these things apply to you, it's time to ask the Lord to help you change. The Lord may be grooming you for your own ministry or leadership position someday, and you want to make sure you are not sowing bad seeds for your future. Or He may want to promote you in other ways. How you serve people is how people will serve you.

STEPS TO KEEPING YOUR HEART RIGHT

1. Pray for your leader and ask for forgiveness.

2. Do not undermine your pastor's decisions.

3. Keep your opinions to yourself unless you are asked by the leadership.

4. Refuse to speak negatively about your pastor, his wife, or his family.

5. Learn to receive correction without feeling attacked or rejected.

6. _____

7. _____

8. _____

9. _____

10. _____

What ways do I see myself falling into the trap of familiarity?	What can I do about it?
1. I allow people to talk negatively to me about my church.	I will point out the positive things about my church.
2. I don't take correction well.	I will meditate on Proverbs 10:17 and 12:1.
3. _____	_____
4. _____	_____
5. _____	_____
6. _____	_____
7. _____	_____
8. _____	_____
9. _____	_____
10. _____	_____

Way 8

Overcome Offenses

We all know that there is no such thing as a perfect church. The best thing to do is look for the good things in your church. Be a part of helping, not complaining. Understand that your church will not always be faultless. Look past its flaws and do your part to make your church better!

There are so many silly little reasons why people get offended. They become offended at the most trivial things. For example, one woman told me that she believed God had called her to attend a certain church — but then later she left because the music was too loud!

I asked her, "Why didn't you just sit in the back or use earplugs, instead of leaving the church that God told you to attend?" Needless to say, she didn't have a good answer to that question! She was just doing what most people do — run when they become offended.

Don't let the devil do that to you. Don't let him run you out of your church because of an offense. God wants you to walk in victory over offenses. He wants you to live completely free from the hurt and turmoil they can cause.

> God wants us to be overcomers in every area of life, and that includes overcoming every offense that comes our way.

We find out how to deal with offenses according to the Word. The Bible assures us that offenses will come to us in this life, but it also tells us we can have the victory over them when they do show up.

Matthew 18:7
Woe unto the world because of offences! for it must needs be that offences come. . . .

However, Jesus goes on to say in John 16:1, *"These things have I spoken unto you, that ye should NOT be offended."* God wants us to be overcomers in every area of life, and that includes overcoming every offense that comes our way.

If something has happened to offend you, pray about your situation; then stand in faith in the midst of it and keep the devil from gaining the upper hand.

Offense Is a Trap

What does it mean to be offended? One dictionary definition of offense is *an act of stumbling; a cause or occasion of sin; a stumbling block.*

In the Bible, the word "offense" comes from the New Testament Greek word "skandalon" — the same Greek word that the English word "scandal" comes from. It refers to the part of a trap to which a bait is attached. In other words, *an offense is a trap that the devil has baited to cause you to stumble and fall!*

Someone in your church may have done something to you or said something about you that caused you to be offended. You may feel hurt and misunderstood, or you may feel resentful and angry toward that person. But no matter how you feel, you will fall into the trap that the devil has set for you if you don't make the decision to let that offense go.

If you allow yourself to focus on an offense that you have suffered, it can become a trap that distracts you from doing what God wants you to do. It can cause you to leave the church that God has told you to attend. But God has made a way in His Word for you to overcome offenses!

Mark 11:25 AMPLIFIED
And whenever you stand praying, if you have any-
thing against anyone, forgive him and let it drop
(leave it, let it go), in order that your Father Who is
in heaven may also forgive you your [own] failings
and shortcomings and let them drop.

God tells us we are to forgive those who have offended us, and then *let it go.* You see, forgiveness is a decision, not a feeling. We can choose to forgive by faith the same way we receive any of God's blessings.

Called for a Reason, Not Just a Season

God has called you to your church for a reason. Your church needs you, and you need your church. You don't want to miss out on the blessings God has for you there by getting offended and leaving.

1 Corinthians 12:18
But now God hath set the members every one of them in the body, as it hath pleased him.

> The devil always works overtime trying to offend you, especially at church, because church is where you are ministered to the most.

Notice the Lord has placed you there *because it pleases Him.* He wants you at your church! The devil always works overtime trying to offend you, especially at church, because church is where you are ministered to the most. Not only that, that is where you can be a blessing and your gifts can be used. If he can get you offended and cause you to leave, you're missing out on the blessings of God and so are the people you were to minister to.

Have you heard the saying that the grass is always greener on the other side? That's what people may think, only to find that when they change churches, they may face the same challenging situations, people, or even something worse! So once you know where God wants you to attend church, you can work through any obstacles or offenses that come your way.

When someone offends you, don't *nurse* it,

don't *rehearse* it,

but *curse* it,

disperse it,

and God will *reverse* it!

10 WRONG REASONS FOR LEAVING YOUR CHURCH

1. My pastor doesn't recognize my gift.

2. I don't have a special seat.

3. My pastor isn't giving me enough attention.

4. The people aren't friendly enough.

5. They don't see my gift.

6. Another church started in town.

7. They don't use me the way they should; I feel like I'm being taken for granted.

8. The services are too long, the Spirit's not moving, etc.

9. I should be up there singing instead of that person.

10. If I were the pastor, I would do things differently.

Areas In Which I've Been Offended	Immediate Steps To Overcome
1. My leader didn't like my idea.	I will not take this personally. I will pray and give it to God.
2. The music is too loud.	I will not sit near the loud-speaker. I will move to the back, use earplugs if I have to, and stop complaining.
3. This book is making me angry. (Smile.)	I will forgive Kate and send her an offering. (Smile again.)
4. _____	_____
5. _____	_____
6. _____	_____
7. _____	_____
8. _____	_____
9. _____	_____
10. _____	_____

Way 9

Speak Faith-Filled Words
Over Your Church

There is power in the words we speak! As a matter of fact, words are so powerful that God created the world by them.

Hebrews 11:3
Through faith we understand that the worlds were framed by the word of God, so that things which are seen were not made of things which do appear.

This scripture tells us that the world was framed with words. We, too, can frame our world around us by the words that we speak. We can frame our world of peace, prosperity, and healing by the words that come out of our mouth. The Scripture also tells us that we are snared by the words of our mouth (Prov. 6:2).

James 3:6 tells us that the tongue can ignite a fire and it can spread. This is true negatively and positively. Just like gossip spreads in a *negative* way, you can spread good things about your church in a *positive* way.

I don't know about you, but it was hearing good things about my church that caused me to want to investigate what was happening there. I showed up once and remained ever since.

Even in Jesus' own meetings, people came as a result of the good things they heard about Him. They heard that cripples were walking, blind eyes were opening, miracles were happening, and lives were being restored. Faith comes by hearing (Rom. 10:17). People need to *hear* of the good things that are happening at your church.

> If you really want to be a blessing, you should speak God's Word over your church on a daily basis.

If you really want to be a blessing, you should speak God's Word over your church on a daily basis. Say out loud that God is giving your pastor wisdom and that all your church's needs are met in abundance with plenty left over to give to others. Confess daily that God's glory is in every service, that souls are being saved, and that your church is a mighty force touching your city and the world.

Here are some scriptures that show us the power of words:

Mark 11:23
For verily I say unto you, That whosoever shall say unto this mountain, Be thou removed, and be thou cast into the sea; and shall not doubt in his heart, but shall believe that those things which he saith shall come to pass; he shall have whatsoever he saith.

Hebrews 10:23

Let us hold fast the profession of our faith without wavering; (for he is faithful that promised.)

Proverbs 6:2

Thou art snared with the words of thy mouth, thou art taken with the words of thy mouth.

Proverbs 16:24

Pleasant words are as an honeycomb, sweet to the soul, and health to the bones.

Proverbs 18:4

The words of a man's mouth are as deep waters, and the wellspring of wisdom as a flowing brook.

Proverbs 18:21

Death and life are in the power of the tongue: and they that love it shall eat the fruit thereof.

FAITH-FILLED WORDS THAT YOU CAN SPEAK OVER YOUR PASTOR AND YOUR CHURCH

1. People receive Jesus in every service — we are a soul-winning church.

2. Miracles, signs, and wonders happen in our church.

3. We have more than enough workers, buildings, vehicles, tools, and money to fulfill God's vision for our church.

4. God uses our church to restore broken hearts and broken lives.

5. Families are put back together, marriages are restored, and lives are transformed in our church.

6. We are a friendly, caring church.

7. Our church is growing, reaching more and more people with the Gospel, and influencing our community.

8. _____

9. _____

10. _____

Create your own list here of faith-filled words to speak over yourself.

1. I am a blessing in my church and everywhere I go.

2. I have favor with my pastor, church leaders, and congregation members.

3. _____

4. _____

5. _____

6. _____

7. _____

8. _____

9. _____

10. _____

Way 10
——

Invite People to Church

Sometimes we overlook this easy way of reaching people. For many years I invited my brother John to church. He always said no, but I kept extending the invitation to him over and over again. One day when I was out of town, he went to church by himself and gave his life to the Lord!

Maybe you've never won someone to the Lord — but if you bring someone to church and he answers the altar call, you won him! Inviting people to church is a great way to be a soul-winner. It is a non-intimidating way to witness. If you can just get them in the service, your pastor can do the rest by leading them to the Lord. Just think, you will share in the reward of their eternal future!

> Inviting people to church is a great way to be a soul-winner.

Make it a habit to invite people to church when shopping at the mall, getting your hair done, or eating at a restaurant. You can be a great blessing by spreading the word about your wonderful church. Make a list of 12 people you will start praying for and invite to church. That could be one person a month. I used to put my neighbors on my list and pray months before I even asked them. They weren't saved but many of them are now! It works!

For example, I remember planting seeds about my church to one neighbor for quite some time. I'd see her while I was walking my dog. When we talked, I wasn't pushy or overwhelming, I just shared with her what a difference my church had made in my life. I wanted to see if I could get her to come without her knowing I was a preacher. I kept inviting her to church and, finally, one day, she came and gave her heart to the Lord!

Be Generous

Another great way to draw people to your church could be by blessing your server with a really good tip when you go to a particular restaurant. My board members would always go out to eat at the same restaurant and the minute the servers saw them come in the door, they would fuss over who got to wait on them, because they were such good tippers!

When dealing with people who don't know the Lord, sometimes you have to win them over first by blessing them or doing something that will make their heart receptive.

After you generously tip someone, then he or she will be more open to hearing about your church. When dealing with people who don't know the Lord, sometimes you have to win them over first by blessing them or doing something that will make their heart receptive.

I've seen this work firsthand many times. When I'm on the road, I've gotten the housekeeper who cleaned my hotel room to come to church, as well as people I've met in airplanes and at airports — fellow passengers, porters, and so forth. I simply tell them what a difference my church has made in my life and in the lives of others. You don't have to be an eloquent speaker or preacher to witness to someone or get them to visit your church.

Sometimes just paying for someone's meal, mowing their lawn, or helping them in some kind way can open the door to them accepting your invitation.

Believe God for Ways To Draw People

A great time to invite unsaved people is around holidays because of the special events usually going on, and people's hearts are more open. Also, you can invite someone to lunch or dinner after church. People love food. I always say, "Bring a sinner to dinner." Of course, don't tell *them* you think they are a sinner!

You can have a part in winning someone to the Lord, just by bringing him or her to church. The Bible says God *will make you* a fisher of men — He will help you.

Mark 1:17
And Jesus said unto them, Come ye after me, and I will make you to become fishers of men.

There are a lot of ways to catch fish. God will give you ideas. He knows what bait to use in catching your particular fish. People are hungry and open to the Gospel. Just keep inviting them, and they will come!

IDEAS OF PEOPLE YOU CAN INVITE TO CHURCH:

Hairdresser

Nail technician

Neighbors

Servers

Store clerks

Co-workers

People at the gym

Porters

Delivery people

Add others:_____

_____

_____

_____

_____

_____

_____

The following are 12 people I'm going to pray for and then invite to church.

1. _____

2. _____

3. _____

4. _____

5. _____

6. _____

7. _____

8. _____

9. _____

10. _____

11. _____

12. _____

Way 11

Be a Consistent Giver

I n this chapter, I would like to talk to you and help motivate you about one of the most exciting ways you can be
a blessing to your church, and that is in the area of giving.

Giving, of course, is done in many different ways. For
example, you can give your time by volunteering, give your
support by attending extra church services and special
meetings, or give by praying for your church, pastor, and
the needs of others in your congregation.

All of these things are a blessing, and you are sowing
powerful seeds that God Himself will reward. Time is a
valuable seed. Why not trust God to multiply your time
back to you for the hours you may plant into helping your
church?

'If You Take Care of My Family,
I'll Take Care of Yours'

Your words of encouragement are seeds too. When you
give encouragement to others, trust that the Lord will send
others to encourage you, your children, or other family
members.

I'll never forget the time I was ministered to along these lines. I travel quite a bit, preaching the Gospel and ministering an average of more than 250 times a year in churches all over the U.S. and abroad. The meetings are wonderful, and I have had the tremendous privilege of leading thousands of people to the Lord each year.

> We never want to become so involved in ministry that we neglect our family.

One day, the devil was trying to make me feel bad about living out of state and not being around my family much. I had moved to another state to attend Bible school and answer God's call to ministry. Immediately after graduation, I hit the road traveling and I have been going non-stop for Jesus ever since!

I am very much a family person, and I missed my parents, brothers, and sister at home, as well as a whole slew of cousins too high to count. (Let me just add a thought here about families. Because I was single, I didn't have my own family to take care of like a married woman would. A wife's responsibility is to minister to her husband and children first. We always must remember there is balance in everything we do, even in being a blessing to our church. We never want to become so involved in ministry that we neglect our family.)

I had been able to visit my family from time to time, but I started feeling guilty for not being around more to minister to them. Even though I knew I was in the will of

God, the devil tried to make me feel bad, especially where my older brother was concerned.

My brother wasn't saved and was heading down the wrong path fast. He was one of those hard cases, if you know what I mean! He had a serious addiction to alcohol, and he also criticized and made fun of me all the time because I had become a preacher.

One day as I was praying about it, the Lord spoke something to my heart. He said, "Kate, if you help take care of My family, I'll take care of yours." Wow! That set me free!

Guess what happened? Not long after that, I received a phone call from my brother while I was out on the road ministering. He called to tell me that he had gotten saved! He went to church that Sunday and gave his life to the Lord. He was also completely delivered from alcohol. He is still delivered all these years later, and loves God with all his heart.

God is so good! I had been sowing seeds for years by leading other people's brothers and sisters to the Lord, and then someone else led my brother to the Lord.

Each time you minister to someone in your church, why not sow it as a seed for your own family? Believe that God will send people to minister to your family members. He will send laborers across their path because you have been a laborer yourself! God will reward your giving to others by causing others to give to you!

The Benefits of Giving

Another way we can really be a blessing to our church is to give financially. It is not my intention to go into great detail along these lines, because in my personal opinion, this subject it best taught in great length and detail by your pastor. I would, however, like to encourage you about the bene-

> A *seed* of nothing will produce a *season* of nothing in our lives.

fits you will reap, both spiritually and naturally, as a result of being a consistent financial giver.

My pastor taught me a powerful truth about giving in every offering. He encouraged our congregation to plant something each time an offering was received, no matter how large or small the amount. He got us in the habit of believing that when we *give* consistently, it will *come back* to us consistently. That goes right in line with the following scripture:

Ecclesiastes 11:1
Cast thy bread upon the waters: for thou shalt find it after many days.

I once heard a minister make a powerful statement. He said, "A *seed* of nothing will produce a *season* of nothing in our lives." In other words, if we want a continual flow of financial blessing and favor in our lives, we should practice planting every time we are able.

Ever since I heard my pastor encourage us along these lines, I began this habit of planting every time I am in church. For me, that's quite often, because I am in churches all the time! I may not always be able to give a huge amount, but just doing *something* and getting in the habit of giving and releasing our faith for a harvest can cause Luke 6:38 to come to pass in our lives in tremendous ways.

Luke 6:38
Give, and it shall be given unto you; good measure, pressed down, and shaken together, and running over, shall men give into your bosom. . . .

In my own life and ministry, I have noticed a more consistent flow of financial favor coming back to me as a result of being a consistent giver. Have you ever heard the saying, "You can't outgive God?" When you sow, He always blesses you back. His Word works!

Plant Seeds for Your Future

When you give, you are sowing seeds of faith for your future. I remember when I had just gotten saved. I was 16 years old and didn't have much money to sow, but I decided to be faithful with what I could do. In my heart, I felt that I would one day have my own ministry, traveling and preaching the Gospel. I knew that in order to fulfill my dream, I would need a lot of money and faithful monthly partners.

I didn't have much money at the time. As a matter of fact, all I had left each month after tithing to my church

> When we sow into God's Kingdom, we are making a deposit into our heavenly bank account.

was $15. But I decided that what was in my hand wasn't enough to be my harvest, so I made it my seed!

I made up my mind to sow into someone else's dream, because I believe that what we help make happen for others, God will make happen for us. So I became a monthly partner with three different ministries. I sent them each $5 a month faithfully as seed for my own future ministry. I believed that if I was faithful, others would be faithful to me one day.

The good news is that now, many years later, I have several faithful monthly supporters who help me spread the Gospel. I believe this is a result of sowing seeds years in advance.

When we sow seeds into God's Kingdom, we are making a deposit into our heavenly bank account. The good news is that we can make withdrawals when we need them most. God said in Philippians 4:19 that He would supply *all* your needs! That's why it doesn't matter if your job lays you off. You have seeds in the ground, and because God is your source, He is able to get you a much better-paying job. I love this scripture:

Malachi 3:10

Bring ye all the tithes into the storehouse, that there may be meat in mine house, and prove me now herewith, saith the Lord of hosts, if I will not open you the windows of heaven, and pour you out a blessing, that there shall not be room enough to receive it.

When God is our source we can have peace no matter what is happening around us. When we give, He has promised to pour His blessings upon us!

Blessed To Be a Blessing

Deuteronomy 8:18

Thou shalt remember the Lord thy God: for it is he that giveth thee power to get wealth, that he may establish his covenant which he sware unto thy fathers, as it is this day.

God wants so much to bless us so that we can be a blessing. Let's face it, the more we prosper, the more we can give. The more we give, the more our church prospers financially. Then our church can be an even greater blessing in our community by feeding the poor, reaching children, and winning more souls to the Lord.

We know that the Gospel is free, but the pipeline that carries it is not. It takes money. I don't know about you, but I want to be a huge blessing to my church. I want to be the one who writes those big checks so I can help reach

more people! How about you? However, the way we will
get to that place is by first doing what we can today. As
you sow your seed, trust God to multiply that seed sown.

Blessings can come in several different ways. They may
come through a raise at work, a business idea, favor in sales,
supernatural deals on things you buy, and so forth. The Bible
says that God may even give you a "witty invention."

Proverbs 8:12
**I wisdom dwell with prudence, and find out knowl-
edge of witty inventions.**

I remember meeting a man who tithed faithfully to his
church. His business was in trou-
ble financially and he didn't
think he would make it long. He
was going to have to "shut
down the shop," so to speak.

> . . . God has ways of
> meeting your needs
> that you haven't even
> thought of yet!

However, his pastor told me
how this man continued to be a faithful tither and giver, in
spite of his circumstances. His pastor prayed with him
about it and encouraged him to keep confessing blessings
over his business because he was a giver. He told him to
keep doing Joshua 1:8.

Joshua 1:8
**This book of the law shall not depart out of thy
mouth; but thou shalt meditate therein day and
night, that thou mayest observe to do according to
all that is written therein: for then thou shalt make**

thy way prosperous, and then thou shalt have good success.

Notice that verse says that meditating the Word will bring you good success. The man decided he would go to work early every day to pray and speak God's word over his finances. After he had done that for about nine months, God gave him an idea. It was a simple invention, and he even had a thought on where to go to present his idea.

To make a long story short, one company really liked his idea and bought it for 1.5 million dollars! Wow! Talk about a turnaround! And the man brought his tithe to church the very next Sunday! My favorite part of the story is after that, his church sowed a seed into my ministry as well! We all got blessed!

Listen, friend, God has ways of meeting your needs that you haven't even thought of yet! Just keep being faithful, and you will be rewarded.

Proverbs 28:20
A faithful man shall abound with blessings.

Proverbs 10:4
He becometh poor that dealeth with a slack hand: but the hand of the diligent maketh rich.

I'll never forgot how blessed I was to hear what two members of my ministry board did each year before going on vacation.

> We never know whose life we are touching through our giving.

We were talking over dinner one night as they were preparing to leave on a two-week vacation. They shared how they always made a point of sowing their tithe early before going on vacation. They told me how they were aware of the fact that their church still had expenses to meet while they were gone, and they didn't want to miss out on being a blessing. Their goal was to always put God first in their finances.

Talk about commitment and being a blessing! I have known this couple for many years, and God has blessed them so much. In fact, not long ago, they moved into their dream home. I'm not surprised — are you?

Matthew 6:33
Seek ye first the kingdom of God, and his righteousness; and all these things shall be added unto you.

Your Giving Changes Lives

Being a minister myself, I know what a difference your giving makes in the lives of others. As a matter of fact, no church, or even ministries like my own, could win souls or reach people if it were not for the generosity of the people who sow faithfully.

I was thinking about the day I gave my life to the Lord at one of Kenneth E. Hagin's meetings. When he came to my hometown of Detroit, Michigan, to hold a crusade, I had never heard about being saved! But I sure heard about it that day! My life was never the same again after that one event. I was forever changed.

You may have heard me share my testimony or read about it in my book, *Conquering Intimidation*. It's quite a story. Basically, my life was a real mess until I met Jesus, and then everything changed as a result of that one meeting! That night, I gave my life to Jesus and answered the call to the ministry. Now I have the wonderful privilege of leading thousands to the Lord myself.

All of that happened because people sowed seed into Brother Hagin's ministry to help make that meeting possible.

Romans 10:14

How then shall they call on him in whom they have not believed? and how shall they believe in him of whom they have not heard? and how shall they hear without a preacher?

Thank God, someone helped send that crusade to my hometown. We never know whose life we are touching through our giving. Your giving is changing lives, and I believe that you will share in the rewards each time a person comes forward in your church on Sunday morning to receive Christ. Your seeds are making an eternal impact.

Giving Blesses Your Pastor

After I was saved, the Lord blessed me with a wonderful church to be a part of after graduating from Bible school. I was there when the church first opened and stayed until I moved back home to be with my family 15 years later. This church is where I learned how to walk in victory in life and ministry because of my wonderful pastors.

Talk about having the best pastors! Wow! I really believe I would not be successful in ministry today had it not been for the great examples and love I received from my pastor and his wife. Words can't even express my deep love for them.

Aren't you thankful to God that your pastor and his wife keep preaching when they may not feel like it? Or that they didn't listen to some discouraging person who may have spoken words of criticism trying to pick them apart? They keep smiling, and you may never know if they are going through a hard time. They keep going when they might be tired.

Why do they do it? Because they care. Your pastor often cares more about others than he cares about himself. That's why I know you want to be a blessing to him and his family in any way you can. That's why I wrote this book, so we could all learn how to be a bigger blessing.

Every Seed Counts

Never belittle your seed. It is precious to the Lord.

My church built a beautiful building to minister more effectively to God's people. At the time, I sowed as much as I could. It didn't seem much to me, but all of us doing our part makes a difference, and the building got built.

Let me encourage you right now. You may feel as though your tithe and your seed is small. But never belittle your seed. It is precious to the Lord. Besides, as you are faithful to continue to sow it, God will grow it.

2 Corinthians 9:6,8
. . . He which soweth bountifully shall reap also bountifully. . . . And God is able to make all grace abound toward you; that ye, always having all sufficiency in all things, may abound to every good work.

TEN BENEFITS OF GIVING

1. God promised to pour out blessings to those who tithe (Malachi 3:10).

2. God promised your barns would be filled (Proverbs 3:9,10).

3. Jesus said that when we give it will come back pressed down and running over (Luke 6:38).

4. You will share in the rewards of every person who comes to Christ at your church.

5. When you get involved in your church's dream, God will get involved in yours.

6. When you sow a seed in the offering, that seed never leaves your life, just your hand. It will come back to you again multiplied.

7. God wanted a family so He planted a seed. His Seed (Jesus) produced a great harvest.

8. For God so loved the world that He *gave!* Giving is a big expression of love (John 3:16).

9. God will take something you have (a seed) to create something you have not (a harvest).

10. When you sow it, God will grow it (2 Corinthians 9:8,10)!

My confessions regarding giving:

I will tithe off every paycheck.

I will meditate God's Word concerning finances.

I will speak words of faith over my seed.

I will believe for the following:

1. $500 extra for the building fund

2. _____ extra for missions

3. _____

4. _____

5. _____

Way 12

Reach Out to Others

One way you can be a blessing to your church is to look outside yourself and reach out. People in the world are searching for answers, and we have the answer — His name is Jesus! Now more than ever, the harvest is ripe. So we should take advantage of every opportunity we have to reach out and help others. We don't

> We don't want to get so caught up in our own little world that we neglect people's needs.

want to get so caught up in our own little world that we neglect people's needs.

When people are going through a hard time, their hearts are more open to receiving the Gospel. If we don't reach them with the Gospel when things are tough, someone will reach them with something else.

One Mother's Story

I know one Christian woman who left her church and joined a cult after her daughter died. Her daughter had cancer, and everyone in the church was rallying around her, encouraging her and visiting her every day. She eventually went home to be with the Lord.

This particular church did really well ministering to the daughter during her illness, but after she died, they dropped the ball in ministering to her mother. They really didn't have any type of program in place to minister to people who were grieving, and no one volunteered to call or check up on her.

About six months later, I ran into the mother at a meeting. I asked how things were going and was utterly astonished when she told me she had changed churches. It wasn't just that she changed churches, it was the new church she changed to that shocked me the most! She had joined a cult. The weirdest thing was, she told me she knew it was a cult. She didn't even agree with their teachings.

I asked her why in the world she would do something like that. She explained that after her daughter died, people from the cult came to visit her every day. They cooked meals for her entire family during the week of the funeral and were extremely kind to her. She felt as though she had a whole new group of friends and people who cared about her, while her other church, filled with the Word and Holy Spirit, did nothing. Boy, were my eyes opened after hearing that!

Be Ready When People Are In Need

When people are vulnerable or grieving, they are open to anyone who reaches out to them. They often join the group that gets to them first. I remember going on a missions trip to Russia after Communism fell. The country was open to receive the Gospel, but it was also open to receive all sorts of other things. I remember preaching in a huge stadium, and thousands of people rushed to the altar to receive Jesus as their Savior.

While we were there, we heard about a cult that was coming to the stadium right after we left. They had all their pamphlets printed and ready to be distributed. It was just a matter of who got there first.

That just goes to show that we need to be wise and ready when people need us. We need to reach out before someone else does.

Ask yourself, "What can I do immediately to reach out to someone in need?" Maybe there isn't a program in your church. Possibly you could be a part of starting one, but until then, find a way you can reach out now to help people who are hurting. Perhaps if Christians had called this woman to check up on her, taken her out to eat, and showed they cared, she wouldn't have joined a cult.

> . . . if you give someone what they can't get anywhere else, they will keep returning.

It's always important to remember that if you give someone what they can't get anywhere else, they will keep returning. That's true with love, attention, encouragement, help, or anything that people need. Reach out and touch somebody and make a difference in their life today.

WAYS I CAN REACH OUT TO OTHERS

1. Call someone; be friendly.

2. Offer help or a meal to a family or neighbor in crisis.

3. Mow a lawn or rake leaves for an elderly person (for free!).

4. Send a get well card or note to cheer up someone.

5. If you haven't seen someone in church, check up on him or her.

6. _____

7. _____

8. _____

9. _____

10. _____

Conclusion —

Tips for Success

Tip #1
How To Find the Right Church
For You and Your Family

Have you ever seen the sign that reads: "Attend the church of your choice this Sunday?" Really, I don't think that's quite the way to do it. Although you do have a choice where to visit when looking for a church for you and you family, I believe we should attend the church of *God's* choice.

Attending church is vitally important. Let's read:

Hebrews 10:25
Not forsaking the assembling of ourselves together, as the manner of some is; but exhorting one another: and so much the more, as ye see the day approaching.

Maybe you have just moved to a new area and you are not quite sure where to attend church. The following are suggestions in helping you find a good church for you and your family.

1. <u>Pray and ask God to lead you to the right church.</u>

This may seem a little simple, but this is the most important. Ask the Lord to lead you to the right place. I have heard some people say that when they walked in the door of their church for the very first time, they just knew that they were home. Others had such peace inside. However, you may not know immediately. You may have to visit several times to actually find out what your church doctrine is. You may need to see if your church can really minister to the needs of your family as well.

2. <u>Find out what the church believes.</u>

Many churches have a bulletin listing their beliefs along with scriptures to back them. Make sure they agree with the Bible. Make sure they share your major beliefs.

One way to find out what the pastor believes is to see what other organizations the church is connected with. Where did the pastor go to Bible school? Who are his favorite preachers? Who is his mentor? Once you find out these things, it will give you an idea of how they believe.

3. <u>Does this church meet the needs of your family?</u>

Does the church have ministry to children and youth? Go visit the children's department. How often do they have services for children? Would they just be babysitting your children, or would they be ministering the Word to them?

4. <u>Look for a common vision.</u>

For example, you may have a real heart for soul-winning. Is this a major thrust in this particular church? If it's not, it may be good for you to find a church that matches your vision. Or if supporting missions is a big deal to you, be sure it's a main thrust of the church. The same with feeding the poor, or reaching children and youth.

I remember once when I was deciding where to attend church, one pastor was a preacher and a teacher. In another church I visited, the pastor was strictly a Bible teacher with lots of Greek and Hebrew in his messages. Many people that I knew loved that kind of ministry, but I received more from inspirational teaching and preaching — it was more exciting to me. Both of those styles are good. It just depends on what's in your heart and what ministers to you the most. That's why God has different ministry gifts, to reach the various personalities of everyone.

Tip #2
Eight Ways To Get the Most out of a Church Service

1. Bring your Bible and take notes. Taking notes helps the message sink in. You can take your notes home and review them during your own personal Bible study time.

2. Pray for the service. You may only have time to do this on your way to church. Ask God to give your pastor utterance in the Holy Ghost (Eph. 6:19). Pray for the music team and for the sound system to work properly. Bind any disturbances

and distractions from taking place in the service. Pray that you and others will be ministered to.

3. Train your flesh to sit still and really pay attention to what's being said! Jesus said to take heed what you hear (Mark 4:24). Go to the bathroom *before* service. Don't get up and move around unless it's an emergency. *Please* do not get up and leave during the altar call. It's distracting for the preacher and for the one that God is dealing with. Souls are being saved — it's the most important part of the service.

4. Buy the tape, CD, or video. When you hear a message that really ministers to you, take it home with you. Most churches record the messages, and you can often take it with you the same day. It's been proven that it takes at least seven times of hearing the same message before it really sinks in. When I find a message I really like, I buy the tape and listen to it every day for weeks. I will take it home and write out notes word for word. I often preach my pastor's messages around the country! (Thanks, Pastor!)

5. Sit close if you can. I don't know about you, but I like to be right up where the action is. It seems easier to receive when you can see someone's face and look into their eyes. It makes you feel like the minister is preaching to you more one-on-one. Besides, there are fewer distractions.

6. Help your pastor by responding and paying attention. If he asks you to raise your hand or say amen, don't just sit there — get involved. You may be bored or tired but try not to show it! Preachers come alive when they look at you and you're smiling or nodding or acting happy. You would be

amazed at what ministers notice you doing during the sermon. I can even tell you what the person on the last row of a big church was doing during my preaching. I notice everything!

7. Don't be a distraction. For example, if you have a medical problem or small children, and you know you could possibly be a distraction, sit in the back. I have a friend who is a baby doctor, and she knows she could get paged at any time, so she sits in the back and sets her phone to the vibrate mode. If you're not on call for your job or you don't have a vibrate mode on your phone, turn it off! Have you heard those annoying phones going off during church? They distract everyone around them.

8. Enter into the praise and worship time. Let the praise and worship be your time to enter into God's Presence. Cast all your care on the Lord during this time. When you do, the pressure and stress you may have experienced throughout the week will begin to lift. You will experience a greater joy praising God with other believers (Ps. 16:11). Let this be your time of thanking God for all He has done in your life and all He is going to do.

Tip #3
10 Ways To Make People Feel Welcome in Your Church

1. Be friendly!
2. Remember how you felt when you first walked into a new church.

3. Ask them questions to show you are interested in them.
4. Invite them back or to a special church function.
5. Include them in your conversation.
6. Invite them to sit with you.
7. Offer to show them around the church.
8. Help them take their children to class.
9. Introduce them to people.
10. Answer any questions they might have and give them a bulletin or visitor's packet.

Tip #4
Some Dos and Don'ts That Will Make You a Blessing

DOS	DON'TS
Do look for the positive.	Don't be a complainer.
Do walk in love.	Don't cause strife.
Do show your pastor support.	Don't act like you know more than he does.
Do show mercy to others.	Don't be easily offended.
Do look around and see who might need your help or a kind word.	Don't think only of yourself.
Do pay attention to the pastor's sermon and try to get the most out of it.	Don't fall asleep in the service.

<u>DOS</u>

Do know where you're called and stay faithful.

Do something now to help in your church.

Do tell your pastor the good points in his sermon.

Do be considerate of others who may also want to talk to your pastor.

Do make it easy for your pastor to maintain his peace and anointing so that the message will be good.

Do be easy to get along with.

Do be trustworthy and keep things confidential.

<u>DON'TS</u>

Don't let the devil tell you the grass is greener at some other church.

Don't wait to get involved.

Don't criticize and critique his messages.

Don't take up all his time talking to him.

Don't dump all your problems on him before he preaches.

Don't be a high-maintenance church member.

Don't be a gossip.

Conclusion

My prayer for you:

Dear Heavenly Father, I come to You in the Name of Jesus, bringing before You my friend who is reading this book. Lord, the fact that they have read this book shows that they are not selfish. They love You and want to help others. May Your anointing come upon them in a greater way to serve in their local church. Heal any hurts they may have experienced in church in times past. Restore any broken relationships and, Lord, help them not to be afraid of getting involved or of being hurt again. Let them see it was the enemy who hurt them, and set them free from all fear now.

Dear friend, I pray for blessing and increase over your life for every act of kindness you have shown. May it come back to you and your family abundantly. I pray that your life will never be the same again as a result of giving of yourself to others. May people see God's love flowing through you in a greater way, and may God's grace and anointing come upon you more powerfully than you have known before, making you a great blessing to your pastor, church, and the Kingdom of God.

Thank You, Lord, for blessing your servant to be a blessing. In Jesus' Name, amen.

About the Author

R ev. Kate McVeigh ministers extensively throughout the
United States and abroad, preaching the Gospel of
Jesus Christ with signs and wonders following. Her out-
reach ministry includes books, teaching tapes, and a daily
radio broadcast, "The Voice of Faith," as well as her weekly
television broadcast, which airs throughout the United
States.

Kate is known as a well-grounded evangelist and
teacher of the Gospel, with a powerful anointing to heal
the sick and win the lost. Through Kate's down-to-earth
and often humorous teaching of the Word, many are moti-
vated to attain God's best for their lives.

To contact Kate McVeigh or to receive a free prod-
uct catalog of other books and ministry materials:

Kate McVeigh Ministries
PO Box 1688
Warren, MI 48090-1688
(586) 795-8885
www.katemcveigh.org

An Important Message

If you have never met Jesus Christ, you can know Him today. God cares for you and wants to help you in every area of your life. That is why He sent Jesus to die for you. You can make your life right with God this very moment and make Heaven your home.

Pray this prayer now:

O God, I ask You to forgive me of my sins. I believe You sent Jesus to die on the Cross for me. I receive Jesus Christ as my personal Lord and Savior. I confess Him as Lord of my life and I give my life to Him. Thank You, Lord, for saving me and for making me new. In Jesus' Name, amen.

If you prayed this prayer, I welcome you to the family of God. Please let me know about your decision for Jesus. I want to send you some free literature to help you in your new walk with the Lord.

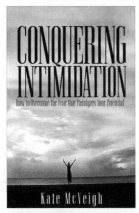

RHEMA
Bible Training Center

Want to reach the height of your potential?

RHEMA can take you there.

- proven instructors
- alumni benefits
- career placement
- hands-on experience
- curriculum you can use

Do you desire —

- to find and effectively fulfill God's plan for your life?
- to know how to "rightly divide the Word of truth"?
- to learn how to follow and flow with the Spirit of God?
- to run your God-given race with excellence and integrity?
- to become not only a laborer but a *skilled* laborer?

If so, then RHEMA Bible Training Center is here for you!

For a free video and full-color catalog, call:
1-888-28-FAITH — Offer #863
(1-888-283-2484)

www.rbtc.org

The Word of Faith is a full-color magazine with faith-building teaching articles by Rev. Kenneth E. Hagin and Rev. Kenneth Hagin Jr.

The Word of Faith also includes encouraging true-life stories of Christians overcoming circumstances through God's Word, and information on the various outreaches of Kenneth Hagin Ministries and RHEMA Bible Church.

To receive a free subscription to *The Word of Faith*, call:
1-888-28-FAITH — Offer #864
(1-888-283-2484)
www.rhema.org/wof